World War II
in 50 Events

From the Very Beginning to the Fall of the Axis Powers

James Weber

World War II In 50 Events

Copyright © 2015 by James Weber

About the Author:

James Weber is an author and journalist. He has a passion for literature and loves writing about social sciences, focusing on history, economics and politics. His hobbies include rowing, hiking and any other outdoor activity. James is married and has two kids.

Other Books in the *History in 50 Events* Series

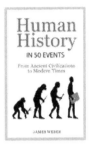

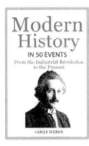

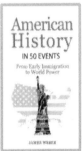

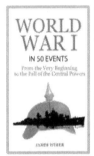

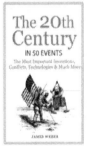

Content

Tensions in Europe Foreshadow the War and First Conflicts in Asia 1

1) September 18, 1931 - Japanese Invasion of Manchuria 2

2) January 30, 1933 - Hitler Becomes German Chancellor 3

3) October 3, 1935 - Italy Invades Ethiopia 5

4) October 25, 1936 - Axis Powers Are Established 6

5) July 7, 1937 - Japan Invades China, Initiating World War II in the Pacific 7

6) May 13, 1938 - Germany Declares Austria Part of the Reich (Anschluss) 9

7) September 29, 1938 - Germany, Italy, Great Britain and France Sign the Munich Agreement 10

8) November 10, 1938 - Kristallnacht Marks First Widespread Hate Act against Jews 11

9) March 31, 1939 - United Kingdom Pledges Support for Polish Independence 12

10) August 23, 1939 - Germany and Soviet Union Sign Non-Aggression Pact 14

From the Beginning of the War to the German Invasion of the Soviet Union 16

11) September 1, 1939 - Germany Invades Poland, Setting Off WWII in Europe 17

12) September 3, 1939 - Britain and France Declare War on Germany 18

13) November 3, 1939 - US Lifts Aid Embargo 19

14) April 9, 1940 - Germany Attacks Denmark and Norway........ 20

15) May 1940 - Germany Seizes Low Countries 21

16) June 10, 1940 - Italy Enters the War....................................... 23

17) June 14, 1940 - The Soviet Union Occupies the Baltic States 24

18) June 22, 1940 - France Surrenders 25

19) September 16, 1940 - US Institutes Peacetime Draft.............. 27

20) October 28, 1940 - Italy Attacks Greece................................ 28

21) October 31, 1940 - Germans Lose Battle of Britain 29

22) March 1, 1941 - Bulgaria Joins the Axis................................. 30

23) June 22, 1941 - Germany Invades Soviet Union 32

The US Enters the War: From Pearl Harbor to the Surrender of Italy

The US Enters the War: From Pearl Harbor to the Surrender of Italy 35

24) December 7, 1941 - Japan Bombs Pearl Harbor. The US Enters the War.. 36

25) December 11, 1941 - Germany Declares War on the US 37

26) May 30, 1942 - The Thousand Bomber Raid Destroys Cologne 38

27) June 7, 1942 - US Wins the Battle of Midway......................... 40

28) October 1942 - Battle of El Alamein Marks Turning Point in Africa 41

29) November 8, 1942 - US and British Troops Invade French North Africa... 42

30) February 2, 1943 - Germans Surrender at Stalingrad.............. 44

31) May 13, 1943 - Axis Forces in Tunisia Surrender to the Allies 45

32) July 10, 1943 - Allied Invasion of Sicily.................................. 46

33) July 25, 1943 - Mussolini Is Deposed...................................... 47

34) September 8, 1943 - Italy Surrenders....................................... 49

The Beginning of the End: From the Invasion of Salerno to the Battle of the Bulge 51

35) September 9, 1943 - Invasion of Salerno 52

36) November 6, 1943 - Kiev Is Liberated By Soviet Troops 53

37) December 1, 1943 - Cairo Declaration 54

38) June 6, 1944 - D-Day 55

39) August 25, 1944 - Liberation of Paris 57

40) October 20, 1944 - US Troops Land in the Philippines 58

41) December 16, 1944 - Battle of the Bulge 59

The Defeat of the Axis: From the Invasion of Germany to the Atom Bomb 61

42) March 7, 1945 - US Troops Cross the Rhine River at Remagen 62

43) April 16, 1945 - Soviets Encircle Berlin 63

44) April 30, 1945 - Suicide of Hitler 64

45) May 7, 1945 - Germany Surrenders to the Western Allies 66

46) May 1945 - Demobilization of American Army Begins 67

47) July 16, 1945 - Atom Bomb Tested in New Mexico 68

48) August 6, 1945 - US Drops Atomic Bomb on Hiroshima 69

49) August 8, 1945 - Soviets Declare War on Japan 70

50) September 2, 1945 - Japan Surrenders 72

Other Books in the History in 50 Events Series**Error!   Bookmark not defined.**

Introduction

World War II was the bloodiest armed conflict in history. With over sixty million military and civilian casualties, it marked the darkest part of the last century. Even today, where most eyewitnesses have already passed away, we can still see the impact the war had on our lives. Today, all of Western Europe consists of democratic countries that have maintained peace with each other throughout the last fifty years. Had the Axis powers won the war, this would certainly not be the case.

This book is meant to help you understand why this war began and how it was fought, and ultimately won, by the Allies. You will see while reading this book that Germany never really had great chances of beating the Allies. Once Hitler decided to invade the Soviet Union and start a two-front war, his Third Reich was doomed. Movies and other media sometimes add to the mystification of the Nazi military, but it should have been clear from the beginning that even Blitzkrieg tactics and Nazi military technology could never beat the Red Army with its over thirty million soldiers.

We can only wish that such a horrible conflict will never take place again. A book such as this one might help pass on the knowledge of our parents and grandparents and teach us (and our kids) about the terrors of war.

James Weber

Tensions in Europe Foreshadow the War and First Conflicts in Asia

1) September 18, 1931 - Japanese Invasion of Manchuria

What many people do not know is that World War 2 began far earlier than 1939 (when Germany invaded Poland). Many historians actually go back to 1931 and the Japanese Invasion of Manchuria, a region in northeast China. Several factors led up to the invasion. Japan was becoming more and more crowded as an island nation due to its rapidly increasing population. Manchuria offered almost 200,000 square kilometers that, once annexed, could easily accommodate the entire Japanese people. Japan also sought after the resources in Manchuria, which included minerals, forestry, and agricultural land. By 1931, Japan's government had invested large sums of money into the economy of Manchuria and the South Manchuria Railway Company. To secure these investments, Japan stationed a large part of its army in the region.

Japanese troops march into the city of Mukden on September 18, 1931

Years later, as the Great Depression hit Japan, many believed their civil government had no solutions to the problems presented by the worldwide depression – possible imperialism became much more popular. Several senior army generals argued for a campaign to win new colonies – especially in China – in order to exploit resources and to regain the power Japanese industries once had. On September 18, 1931, Japanese soldiers invaded Manchuria after claiming that the Chinese had sabotaged the Japanese rail tracks. By February 1932, the Japan army had conquered the entire region of Manchuria and set up a Japanese-controlled state called Manchukuo, run by the former Emperor of China. The League of Nations suggested economic sanctions, which never became effective since the US (Japan's main trading partner) was not a member and Britain had big interest in continuing trade with Japan.

2) January 30, 1933 - Hitler Becomes German Chancellor

January 30, 1933, marked an important turning point for Germany and, eventually, for the world. On this day, German President Paul von Hindenburg named Adolf Hitler, decorated World War I veteran and leader of the Nazi Party, the new chancellor of Germany. Hindenburg initially refused to make him chancellor, intimidated by Hitler's growing popularity and open support for drastic violence. Instead, he decided to appoint General Kurt von Schleicher, an action that led to re-elections.

During the new elections, the Nazis lost ground. Within the next days, which included complicated negotiations, the former German

Chancellor Franz von Papen, supported by several businessmen, convinced Hindenburg to yield and nominate Hitler as chancellor.

Hitler after his inauguration as chancellor

At the time of Hitler's rise, Germany was a nation that had little experience with democracy. Shortly after World War I, the Weimarer Republik was founded – the first German democracy. It was soon plagued by indecisive and self-serving elections and politicians, which further demoralized the people's belief in the system. Most of the population was unemployed, without food, and desperate for relief. His plan, supported by the majority of the Germans, was to strengthen the country through a one-party state. Measures included the expansion of the police state, as well as rearming the military forces.

3) October 3, 1935 - Italy Invades Ethiopia

In 1935, the League of Nations had to face another crucial test. Italy, under the rule of fascist dictator Benito Mussolini, invaded the African country of Abyssinia (now Ethiopia) on the horn of Africa. Mussolini justified this step as being no different from actions of other colonial powers in Africa. Italy's reason for invading the country were not only its resources, but also national prestige. In 1896, the Abyssinian military defeated Italy in what is known as the Battle of Adowa.

Italian soldiers leaving for Ethiopia

The two countries clashed again in December 1934 at the Wal-Wal Oasis on the border between Abyssinian Somaliland, where 200 soldiers from both sides lost their lives. Mussolini felt that Abyssinia should be held accountable for the incident and used it as propaganda to gain support for an invasion by his people. Many saw it as a possibility to provide land for unemployed Italians and acquire more mineral resources to fight off the effects of the Great Depression.

4) October 25, 1936 - Axis Powers Are Established

The Axis powers grew before and during the war, beginning with a treaty of friendship signed by Germany and Italy on October 25, 1936. One week after the signing, Mussolini declared that all other European countries would from then on rotate on the Rome-Berlin axis, thus creating the term "Axis." As a second step, Germany and Japan signed the Anti-Comintern Pact, an anti-communist treaty, which Italy joined in 1937. In general, the Axis members had two common interests. First, the territorial expansion and foundation of empires based on military conquest, as well as the overthrow of the post-World War I international order. Second, the destruction or neutralization of Soviet Communism.

The signing of the Tripartite Pact by Germany, Japan, and Italy in Berlin

However, it was only in 1939 when the alliance became of importance, when Germany invaded Poland. The so-called "Pact of Steel" was established, which guaranteed help in case one of the pacts members declared war on another country. Even though there were no official meetings between Germany, Japan, and Italy after 1940, the Axis presided over territories that occupied large parts of Europe, North Africa, and Asia, with its largest extension around 1942/1943. After the surrender to the Allied power, the Axis alliance was dissolved in 1945.

5) July 7, 1937 - Japan Invades China, Initiating World War II in the Pacific

After the Japanese invasion of the Chinese region of Manchuria, tensions between the two countries reached new heights. Though smaller in manpower, Japan was the stronger military power. Its political and economic development during the beginning of the 20th century stood in stark contrast to that of China. Industrialization and trade with the West had propelled Japan into the modern world, while China still consisted of mostly poor farmers and an untrained military.

Japanese troops entering China

The full-scale war between the two began on July 7, 1937, after Japanese troops opened fire on local soldiers at Marco Polo Bridge near Beijing. Though diplomats from both sides signed a ceasefire, the two countries increased military numbers in the region. In late July, Japan decided to declare war on China and invade the country with its full power. Chinese armies attempted to resist the invasion, but were quickly overrun by the technological supremacy and preparedness of its counterpart. As the Chinese military had no tanks and only a few aircrafts, the first phase of the war was more of a blitzkrieg of Japanese than an even war. More than 500,000 Japanese troops moved against Shanghai, Nanjing, and mainland China, while Japanese military planes bombarded regions where their infantry could not penetrate. In late 1937, the Chinese government was forced to retreat further into the mainland and moved its capital to Chongqing.

6) May 13, 1938 - Germany Declares Austria Part of the Reich (Anschluss)

Even though Germany and Austria share the same language, both countries always showed great differences in culture and mentality. After the Austro-Prussian War of 1866 resulted in the dissolution of the 19th-century German Confederation, there were only loose associations between Austria and the various independent German monarchies. When Hitler annexed Austria in 1938, it was clear that he disobeyed the Treaty of Versailles, which forbade a unification of the two countries after World War I.

German and Austrian police taking down a border post.

The German army then crossed the border into Austria and quickly assumed control of the country, taking it from Chancellor Kurt Schuschnigg. Most Austrians favored this move, as they believed it meant more international influence for their country. No real objections were raised by neighboring countries like Italy, which had, to that point, stood between the two nations, or even by France and England. It should have become obvious after taking Austria, and later the Sudetenland, that Hitler's Third Reich would continue to expand.

7) September 29, 1938 - Germany, Italy, Great Britain and France Sign the Munich Agreement

Before the Munich Agreement, Hitler threatened to take over the Sudetenland by force if the great European powers did not hand it to him. In a private meeting at his home in Berchtesgaden, the dictator told British Prime Minister Chamberlain about his plans, who almost instantly dismissed them as unacceptable. Hitler appealed to Chamberlain's unwillingness to go to war with Germany and suggested a four-way conference between Germany, Britain, Italy, and France – an idea he got from Mussolini.

Hitler and Chamberlain in Munich

The meeting was to take place in Munich on September 29, 1938. In an effort to avoid war, Neville Chamberlain and French Prime Minister Edouard Daladier suggested that the Third Reich have the Sudetenland, a decision that is now considered one of the greatest failures in appeasement policy. Hitler promised not to invade any other territory in Europe. Reactions to the agreement were positive, as the British thought they had avoided war with Germany. Nevertheless, politicians such as Winston Churchill criticized the agreement, since giving in to Germany would mean losing the support of the Czech Army, which many considered one of the best in the region. In March 1939, the German Army took over what was left of Czechoslovakia, which broke the Munich Agreement and raised doubts about the possibility of a peaceful compromise.

8) November 10, 1938 - Kristallnacht Marks First Widespread Hate Act against Jews

The Kristallnacht was the first massive and coordinated attack against Jews throughout the German Reich on the night of November 9, 1938. Leading up to the event, Herschel Grynszpan, a German Jew, shot and killed a member of the German Embassy staff in an act of retaliation for the poor treatment his family suffered at the hands of the Nazis in Germany. His family and about

15,000 other Jews, originally from Poland, had been expelled from Germany on October 27. Like cattle, they were forced into trains and later dumped at the Polish border.

Smashed windows the day after Kristallnacht

For the Nazis, the shooting in Paris provided an opportunity to rally up Germans against the Jews. Newspapers and other media reported about the shooting without mentioning the background story. On November 9, throughout many cities in the Third Reich, mob violence broke out with members of the SS and Hitler Youth beating several Jews to death and destroying houses and businesses. The shattered window glass gave the night its name Kristallnacht (crystal night). As shops and synagogues were burning, most police officers and fire departments stood by and watched.

9) March 31, 1939 - United Kingdom Pledges Support for Polish Independence

On March 31, 1939, after Hitler had occupied Czechoslovakia and therefore disobeyed the Munich Agreement, the United Kingdom pledged support to guarantee Polish independence. It was stated that in the event of a threat to the Polish country that demanded military force, Britain would support Poland and its borders. A week later, during a visit to London by the Polish foreign minister, it was agreed to formalize this guarantee in an Anglo-Polish military alliance.

Poland before the war

At the time of the guarantee, Adolf Hitler was making further territorial demands against Poland. He expected a cession of the port of Danzig, an extraterritorial highway (the Reichsautobahn Berlin-Königsberg) across the Polish Corridor, as well as special privileges for the German minority within Poland. Poland rejected the German demands and would be invaded half a year later.

10) August 23, 1939 - Germany and Soviet Union Sign Non-Aggression Pact

On August 23, 1939, foreign minister of Nazi Germany, Joachim von Ribbentrop, and Soviet foreign minister Vyacheslav Molotov signed a non-aggression pact, which would seal the fate of millions of people. As stated in the document, both countries promised not to interfere in case the other went to war. At the same time, a second, secret agreement was made that divided eastern Europe (especially Poland) between the two totalitarian states.

German and Soviet troops meet in Poland

The pact kicked-off World War II, as the Nazis no longer had to fear the "red giant" to the east. Just days after signing the two pacts, and confident that the Soviets would not oppose, Germany invaded Poland. Several weeks later, the Soviet Union invaded Poland from the east to take its share of the country. In the following months, it also occupied Estonia, Latvia, Lithuania, and the Romanian province of Bessarabia. Though Britain and France protested, they could not afford to fight Stalin as well, since their forces were already facing Germany.

James Weber

From the Beginning of the War to the German Invasion of the Soviet Union

11) September 1, 1939 - Germany Invades Poland, Setting Off WWII in Europe

During the morning hours of September 1, 1939, more than one and a half million German soldiers crossed the Polish border by air and by land. The invasion was part of Hitler's "blitzkrieg" strategy, in which the enemy was basically overrun. Planes, tanks, and air forces were deployed as fast as possible, and troops destroyed railroads and all means of communication. The German infiltrated strongholds by posing as Polish military officers, and killed enemies with explosives, guns, and even sabers.

A Polish city destroyed by German bombs

Officially, the attack was meant as a response to Polish shots on German territory. It is now known that these claims made by Hitler before the Reichstag were false, and that the initial Polish attack was staged by disguised German troops. Poland's army was completely unprepared for the blitzkrieg tactics and surrendered within weeks. Even though it numbered about 700,000 soldiers, the Polish infantry was trained for the slow trench warfare of World War I. There was no way the army could deploy its troops quickly enough to defend against the more powerful German forces.

12) September 3, 1939 - Britain and France Declare War on Germany

In response to the German invasion of Poland, Britain demanded that Hitler withdraw his troops from the country immediately. After he declined to respond, both Britain and France declared war on Germany to honor their obligations as allies of Poland. Along with the British and as part of the United Kingdom, Australia, New Zealand, and India also declared war on the Third Reich.

Newspaper announcing the beginning of the war

The first casualty was the British ocean liner *Athenia*, which was shot by a German submarine. Germany later claimed that the liner was armed. Of the 1,100 passengers on board, 112 died. Even though 28 of them were Americans, President Roosevelt declared that the US would not send troops to Europe and maintain neutrality. Britain then began bombing German ships on September 4, though suffering significant losses. The soldiers were ordered not to harm German civilians, a restriction that the German military never faced. France would attack Germany's western border two weeks later, an effort that was weakened due to the path leading to the German front being enclosed by the borders of Luxembourg and Belgium. As both were neutral countries, the French military could not cross their borders and had to use the narrow passage.

13) November 3, 1939 - US Lifts Aid Embargo

The US Congress passed the so-called Neutrality Acts in 1935 and 1936, which restricted the sale of arms and war materials to European countries. The bill was meant to further underline American neutrality and its isolationist sentiment. In 1939, with threats to democracy in Western Europe rising, President Franklin D. Roosevelt sought to ease these restrictions. He addressed Congress and warned about a second global conflict if no help was given to democratic countries. He stated that the old American neutrality laws would indirectly benefit aggressor countries, while denying aid to victimized nations.

Protester's sign against US involvement in Europe

He proposed new laws that allowed the purchase of arms and goods from the US. Technically, this regarded any country, but Roosevelt's goal was to supply Britain and France so they could keep up with Germany's superior military. Changes also included the ban on American ships from transporting arms or war material and prohibiting American citizens to travel on ships from belligerent nations. Congress agreed to the proposed changes on November 3, 1939. This was an important step for Britain, as it would soon be the last bastion against Nazi Germany in Europe.

14) April 9, 1940 - Germany Attacks Denmark and Norway

Germany's assault on Denmark and Norway were codenamed "Operation Weserübung," meaning Operation Weser-Exercise, with the Weser being a German river. On April 9, 1940, Germany invaded Denmark and Norway in order to prevent a possible Franco-British occupation of Norway. Both Denmark and Norway were informed that this was an act of protection against Allied aggression.

A German tank invading Denmark

Denmark's army surrendered almost immediately, as military generals and the Danish King Christian X were convinced that fighting the German would result in a slaughter of their people. This was not the case for Norway, which continued to fight alongside British troops. Hitler responded with a parachute invasion and the installation of a puppet regime led by Vidkun Quisling, a pro-fascist former foreign minister who helped German troops take over his country after Britain had to transfer most of its troops to France.

15) May 1940 - Germany Seizes Low Countries

An assault on the Low Countries, which included Holland, Belgium, and Luxemburg, was the logical next step in Hitler's plan to take over Europe. On May 10, 1940, German troops crossed the Dutch border in the now familiar Blitzkrieg fashion. The main cities were quickly overrun, as dive-bombers destroyed the Dutch air force and German infantry followed tanks across the country. Holland's Royal Family escaped to England, and the country officially surrendered on May 15, 1940, five days after the initial attack. Luxembourg and Belgium were attacked on the same day as Holland, with only Belgium being able to mount a real defense. French and British Allied forces on the continent moved toward Belgium as fast as possible, but were unable to avoid the defeat. On May 25, King Leopold of Belgium notified Britain that his country would soon have to surrender.

A Royal Navy ship covering retreating troops at Dunkirk

Although the speed and force of the German army clearly surprised the Allies, Britain managed to execute one of the most important military maneuvers in history, in what is now known as the Dunkirk evacuation. It sent every civilian and military craft afloat in Britain across the English Channel. While the Germans were held at bay by the Royal Navy and a defensive perimeter on land, over 338,000 men – including 140,000 French and Belgians – were evacuated to

England over a period of only nine days. Even though many tanks were lost, the soldiers lived to fight another day, a moral victory that baffled the Germans, who believed their enemy's troops were hopelessly trapped.

16) June 10, 1940 - Italy Enters the War

Though Italy's decision to go to war against Britain and France seemed logical, due to its Axis pact with Germany, Benito Mussolini wanted to make sure to enter the war on the side of the victorious. It was likely that France would collapse any day and many believed Britain would soon follow. Germany's military strength convinced Mussolini that he could win the war without too much risk. Italy had long wanted to expand its Empire and take over British territories.

Mussolini declaring war on Britain and France in Rome

The goal was to eliminate the Anglo-French domination in the Mediterranean, recapture old Italian territory, and expand of Italian influence over the Balkans and in Africa. Italy declared war on France and Britain on the evening of June 10. At first, the two sides exchanged only air raids as both France and Italy adopted a defensive posture along their borders. However, when Italian troops entered France a few days later, it destroyed all hope of the Allies to win back the country.

17) June 14, 1940 - The Soviet Union Occupies the Baltic States

The Molotov-Ribbentrop Pact signed between Germany and the Soviet Union in 1939 declared Estonia and Latvia as part of the Soviet Union, while Lithuania would belong in the sphere of influence of the Germans. After the invasion of Poland, territories were exchanged, and eventually all of the Baltic States fell to the Soviets. During the following invasion by the Red Army in the summer of 1940, Soviet authorities compelled the Baltic governments to resign.

Monument to Lithuanian victims of Soviet occupation

Many high officials were imprisoned and later died in Siberia. Soon after, Soviet-friendly politicians were placed at the top of the governments in the Baltic States. The occupation lasted until June 1941, when Germany attacked the Soviet Union and captured the countries. At this point, many civilians actually believed the Germans to be liberators.

18) June 22, 1940 - France Surrenders

After the evacuation of many British and French soldiers at Dunkirk, the German advance continued to sweep southward. Faced with a sheer unstoppable enemy, not only the French army retreated, but an estimated 10 million civilians, many of them from the capital. With the Germans closing in, France declared Paris an open city. This allowed Hitler to enter the French capital on June 14 without any kind of resistance.

Hitler standing in front of the Eifel Tower

Although a new ad-hoc government was quickly formed with French World War I hero Marshall Petain as its leader, his only real action as head of the French was to tell his countrymen that he was about to surrender to the Germans. The French government then called on the Germans for an armistice in order to end the bloodshed. Hitler decided that the French capitulation was to take place at Compiegne, a forest north of Paris, as this was the same place the Germans had signed the armistice ending World War I twenty-two years earlier. The location was chosen to disgrace the French and avenge the

German loss. The armistice was signed on June 22. Under its terms, two-thirds of France was to be occupied by the Germans. In addition, France had to disband its army and bear the cost of the German invasion.

19) September 16, 1940 - US Institutes Peacetime Draft

With the war in Europe progressing, the US took first preparations in case the Americans were dragged into the conflict. On September 16, 1940, Congress instituted the Selective Training and Service Act, which required all men between the ages of 21 and 45 to register for the draft. It was the first peacetime draft in the country's history. Those who were selected from the draft lottery were required to serve at least one year in the armed forces. Should the US enter the war, the terms would be extended through the duration of the fighting. Until the end of the war in 1945, 50 million men had registered for the draft, with 10 million inducted in the military forces.

Franklin D. Roosevelt signing the Act

Although the United States was still officially neutral, many people thought that an intervention would be needed eventually. Great Britain's chances to defeat Germany on its own seemed to decrease as the Nazis gained more and more ground on the continent. Since the American military was unprepared to fight a global war in 1939 and 1940, many saw a draft and increase in military spending as a necessary evil. Over time, national polls showed a growing majority in favor of the Congress' decision.

20) October 28, 1940 - Italy Attacks Greece

On October 28, 1940, Mussolini ordered one of the most disastrous military campaigns of the war. The Italian dictator surprised everyone – even his own generals – with his move against Greece. As soon as he heard about it, Hitler denounced the attack, because he believed the Italian troops were badly needed in Africa. He turned out to be right.

Defensive trench construction made by Greek soldiers

The Greek military was able to defend against the Italians, even pushing them back into Albania after just one week. Mussolini had underestimated their fighting power, as well as the mountainous Greek terrain, which was a lot easier to defend than to attack. Even though he had put aside millions of Lire to bribe Greek politicians and generals not to resist the Italian invasion, the money never made it past his own bureaucracy. In order to prevent the Greeks from embarrassing the Italian military even further, Hitler moved many of his men from several battlefields to Greece. Although the Axis later captured the small country, it had immensely ridiculed Mussolini.

21) October 31, 1940 - Germans Lose Battle of Britain

After taking most of western Europe, Hitler was eager to invade Britain. "Operation Sealion" would have the Luftwaffe attempt to gain air control, before infantry could cross the English Channel via boats. German military officials were confident that their planes could easily beat the British. In 1939, Germany had 4,000 aircrafts compared to Britain's front-line strength of 1,660, with the main fighter planes being the Messerschmitt fighters and their Junkers dive-bombers (Germany) and the Spitfire and the Hurricane (Great Britain). Unexpectedly, the Germans met heavy resistance from British fighters, which had the advantage of being able to land and reload anytime.

An example of a Hawker Hurricane R4118, which fought in the Battle of Britain.

Over the next weeks, Hitler would launch several air strikes against major industries and even cities. However, the Royal Air Force managed to regain air superiority and by October 31, British generals were confident that there would be no land invasion in 1940. However, the bombings continued, and would eventually result in nearly 40,000 civilian deaths. The defeat of the Germans at the Battle of Britain marked the first major turning point of the war.

22) March 1, 1941 - Bulgaria Joins the Axis

Like Italy, Bulgaria wanted to make sure to join the victorious side when entering the war. It had lost World War I alongside the Central Powers (Austria-Hungary and the German Empire) and could not repeat this mistake. When World War II broke out, the Bulgarian government declared its neutrality at first. As German forces swept over Europe, many were impressed by Hitler's Blitzkrieg tactics and believed he was about to win the war.

Picture of the Bulgarian Army

Eager to expand his territory, King Boris of Bulgaria then decided to join the Axis and hoped, with the help of his new allies, to gain access to the Aegean by claiming Greek territory to the Bulgarian south. On March 1, the Germans came marching through the Balkans as the Bulgarian king signed the Tripartite Pact in Vienna. Bulgaria benefited from the alliance in the short term, as it made territorial gains in both Greece and Yugoslavia. Nonetheless, after German soldiers attacked the Soviet Union and later lost in Stalingrad (we will come to that later), Bulgaria was captured by the USSR and a pro-Soviet government was installed.

23) June 22, 1941 - Germany Invades Soviet Union

In July 1940, only weeks after the Germans invaded France and the Low Countries, Hitler decided to fight a two front war and attack the Soviet Union within the following year. Some historians regards this move as his biggest mistake during the war. Under the codename "Operation Barbarossa," German troops invaded the Soviet Union on June 22, 1941, less than two years after their non-aggression pact was signed. The operation included three million German soldiers, backed up by more than half a million troops from Axis allies.

German cannons preparing for the invasion

Hitler had always intended to attack the Soviet Union and saw their non-aggression pact as merely a tactical maneuver. His goal was to wipe out the communist state as well as all Russian Jews, whom he believed to be the racial basis for the Soviet state. The invasion would be the largest German military operation of World War II, despite the Soviet Army outnumbering the Wehrmacht by far. German generals planned another surprise, as their Blitzkrieg tactic had worked well in Western Europe. Their plan worked at first, and the Soviet armies acted overwhelmed. Front units encircled most of the Soviet soldiers and cut them off from supplies and reinforcements. Most times, all they could do was surrender.

The US Enters the War:From Pearl Harbor to the Surrender of Italy

The US Enters the War:From Pearl Harbor to the Surrender of Italy

24) December 7, 1941 - Japan Bombs Pearl Harbor. The US Enters the War

In the morning hours of December 7, 1941, the Japanese launched a surprise torpedo attack on the US Naval Base Pearl Harbor in Hawaii. Vice-Admiral Chuichi Nagumo ordered close to 360 Japanese warplanes to attack more than thirty American ships. The US sustained a loss of 170 aircrafts that morning, as well as 18 ships. Around 3,600 Americans lost their lives that day, with only very few Japanese casualties.

USS *Arizona* on the day of the attack

Japan had several reasons for the attack. Emperor Hirohito long wanted to expand his territory and power like European countries. In search for natural resources, the US was a likely target and also presented a formidable barrier between Java's oil fields and Japanese fleets. On the Asian continent, Japan could not conduct military strategies against the Netherlands and territories of the United Kingdom with a strong American presence. Following the attacks, President Franklin D. Roosevelt delivered a speech on December 8, also known as the "Infamy Speech," informing Congress and the American public that the attack happened while the US was in the midst of talks to keep peace. On that same day, America entered World War II.

25) December 11, 1941 - Germany Declares War on the US

The attacks on Pearl Harbor came as a surprise even to Germany. Although the country had agreed to help defend Japan in case of war, the Tripartite Pact stated no obligation to fight a war if Japan itself was the aggressor. Following the attacks, Japanese Ambassador Oshima tried to nail down German Foreign Minister von Ribbentrop on a formal declaration of war against America. Von Ribbentrop hesitated, as he feared that another antagonist, such as the powerful United States, would be too much even for the German military.

Hitler declaring war on the United States in Berlin

Hitler thought otherwise. He famously underestimated the US and believed their military would soon be beaten by the Japanese. He also saw an American declaration of war on Germany as inevitable. There is still a lot debate among historians as to whether this was true or not. Even though a big majority of Americans favored a war against Japan, many did not share those sentiments in the case of Germany. Former German immigrants made up a big part of the American population, and Roosevelt had never planned to fight an all-out war in the Pacific as well as in Europe.

26) May 30, 1942 - The Thousand Bomber Raid Destroys Cologne

The British had flown bomber attacks on German cities since the beginning of the war. In 1942, they decided to target major German cities in order to destroy civilian morale. The most notable raid took place during the night of May 30, 1942, over Cologne. The city had been chosen as the ideal target because it was reasonably near for the British planes in terms of flying and, as a major railway hub, its destruction could seriously damage Germany's ability to transport goods.

Cologne after the war

Bomber took off at 10:30 PM from over fifty bases across Britain. Pilots were told to seek out the River Rhine when flying over Germany, following it until they reached Cologne. Once the first bombers arrived, they dropped their bombs over the city's old town. Part of the plan was to light it up with incendiary bombs, which would help other bombers find their targets. They would then bomb areas in every direction one mile from the city's Neumarkt. The plan worked, and within fifteen minutes of the first bombs exploding, most of the town was destroyed.

27) June 7, 1942 - US Wins the Battle of Midway

Only half a year after the Japanese attacks on Pearl Harbor, one of the most decisive battles of the Pacific theater of the war would be fought in the waters around the Midway Islands. In a battle that would last four days, the US Navy managed to destroy four Japanese aircraft carriers while losing only one American carrier. This marked an important victory over the Japanese navy, which was thought of as invincible before.

The Midway Islands, located in the Pacific halfway between Japan and the US

Prior to the battle, the Japanese fleet had made huge advancements in the Pacific. The small but strategic island of Midway would become the focus of their plan to destroy the US Pacific fleet. Japanese generals wanted to lure the Americans into a trap. They would invade

40

Midway, and once US ships arrived to respond to the invasion, they could be destroyed by the larger Japanese fleet hidden to the west. What they did not know was that US intelligence had broken the Japanese naval code, and the Americans had already worked out a plan to counter-maneuver the surprise attack. To avoid the trap, two US attack fleets caught the Japanese force entirely by surprise and destroyed three heavy Japanese carriers and one heavy cruiser. Japan's losses ended its sea superiority and made an American counteroffensive possible that did not cease until Japan's surrender three years later.

28) October 1942 - Battle of El Alamein Marks Turning Point in Africa

In 1941, the war had entered Africa. The Germans were fighting the British over most of North Africa and had enjoyed great success. By the summer of 1942, they seemed to have captured Europe almost entirely. In order to stop them, Britain needed to make sure they would not expand their territory even further. For them, the war in the desert of North Africa was pivotal. If the German Afrika Korps secured the Suez Canal, the ability of the Allies to supply themselves would be severely dented. The only other option available was a supply route via South Africa – both longer and more dangerous.

British Crusader Mk I tanks

The Battle of El Alamein was primarily fought between two of the genius commanders of World War II, Bernard Montgomery and Erwin Rommel. Rommel commanded about 100,000 men and five hundred tanks, while Montgomery led more than double the number of tanks and men, made up of British, Australians, New Zealanders, Indians, and South Africans. Allied air superiority stood at about the same proportion. The Battle began on October 23, and the result after ten days of ferocious pounding was complete Allied victory, which led to the retreat of the Afrika Korps and the German surrender in North Africa in May 1943.

29) November 8, 1942 - US and British Troops Invade French North Africa

The invasion of French North Africa, named "Operation Torch," was planned for November 1942. US and British forces carried out the campaign, in which three task forces were to land on the beaches near Casablanca on the Moroccan Atlantic Coast, near Oran in western Algeria and near Algiers, more than 250 miles to the east in Algeria.

British Spitfires fighter being assembled in North Africa

From North Africa, the plan was to invade Sicily, later mainland Italy, and then move up to northern Europe. Victory in the region would also do a great deal to clear the Mediterranean Sea of Axis shipping and leave it more unrestricted for the Allies to use. The invasion proved successful and triggered a rapid dispatch of German troops to Southern France, which would later become important, as these troops would be missing during the fight against the Soviets on the eastern front. By the end of November, the Allies had crossed the Tunisian border in the northwest.

30) February 2, 1943 - Germans Surrender at Stalingrad

Many consider the Battle of Stalingrad the major turning point of World War II in Europe. It stopped the German advance into the Soviet Union and changed the war in favor of the Allies. Unfortunately, it was also one of the bloodiest battles in history, with combined military and civilian casualties of nearly two million. Leading up to the battle, the Germans saw the conquest of Stalingrad as essential to their campaign in southern Russia, since it was strategic point on the Volga River. Nevertheless, Stalin was determined to defend the city at all costs, since he knew of the symbolic importance of the city that bore his name.

Soviets preparing to fight off a German assault

In September 1942, the Sixth Army advanced on the city of Stalingrad. Their primary task was to secure the oil fields in the Caucasus close to Stalingrad. Until then, the Germans had never been defeated in Russia, but in mid-November, after reaching the city, the invaders were running short of men and munitions. The Russians then launched a counteroffensive to encircle the enemy. Although most likely able to fight their way out, German soldiers were forbidden to leave the city. Hitler had ordered to defend Stalingrad at all costs. As winter set in and with no rescue in sight, more and more soldiers were freezing and starving. On February 2, 1943, Wehrmacht General Paulus surrendered what was left of his army. About 150,000 Germans had died in the fighting.

31) May 13, 1943 - Axis Forces in Tunisia Surrender to the Allies

The Africa Operation ended when over 230,000 Axis forces surrendered during May 1943. Leading up to the event, the Afrika Korps had suffered great losses at El Alamein, and morale was rapidly decreasing. On May 9, 12,000 Germans laid down their weapons after being cornered by American troops. About 22,000 Germans in the mountainous Zaghouan sector also stopped fighting two days later. Reports of several German division giving up continued throughout the next few days. Even Von Arnim's infamous elite divisions from Europe no longer wanted to fight to the bitter end.

US troops and abandoned German equipment

Unlike the Germans, many Italian troops kept fighting, even with less supplies and equipment, and Italian General Messe vowed to fight until the last man. Many regarded Tunisia as an outpost of their own country, a sentiment that the Germans did not share. When Mussolini heard about the imminent collapse of the German troops and the hopeless situation his troops were in, he personally gave Messe orders to surrender.

32) July 10, 1943 - Allied Invasion of Sicily

After the Allies had defeated Axis forces in the North African Campaign, they looked ahead to the invasion of occupied Europe and the final defeat of Nazi Germany. They decided to move against Italy next, in order to remove Mussolini and his fascist regime from the war. The Italy Campaign began with the invasion of Sicily in July 1943, with its codename "Operation Husky."

An American tank in Sicily

Attacks began on July 10, 1943, including air strikes and sea landings with more than a hundred thousand troops, three thousand ships, and four thousand aircrafts. The invasion was nearly cancelled the day before, when bad weather caused problems for paratroopers trying to drop off behind enemy lines. British generals decided to advance anyway, as they believed that German forces along the Sicilian coast would never anticipate enemy landings in such rain and wind. The landings advanced as planned, as Allied troops encountered little resistance to their attacks. After 38 days of fighting, the US and Great Britain successfully drove German and Italian troops from Sicily and prepared to assault the Italian mainland.

33) July 25, 1943 - Mussolini Is Deposed

On July 25, 1943, Italian dictator Benito Mussolini was voted out of power by his own Grand Council. Leading up to the event, the Allied invasion of Sicily and catastrophic losses on the Italian side had weakened Mussolini's position. It now became obvious to just about everyone that the country had backed the losing side and was heading for a military catastrophe.

Picture of Mussolini

In the early hours of July 25, the government's Council met to discuss the future of their country. Dino Grandi, a Council member, proposed a vote to transfer some of Mussolini's power back to the king. Years earlier, this proposal would have landed Grandi in prison or had him hanged. Surprisingly, the motion was passed, with Mussolini barely reacting. He was then called for a meeting with King Victor Emmanuel III., who told him that the war was lost. Upon leaving the meeting, Mussolini was arrested by the police, who had been secretly planning to remove him for quite some time. When news of Mussolini's arrest was made public, most Italians felt relieved, convinced that the worst was over.

34) September 8, 1943 - Italy Surrenders

Only six weeks after Mussolini had been sent to prison, General Dwight Eisenhower publicly announced the surrender of Italy to the Allies. Mussolini's deposing meant the collapse of the fascist government in Italy. Pietro Badoglio, who was placed as a substitute, began negotiating with the Allies shortly after. A conditional surrender was approved, which allowed the Allies to land in southern Italy in what would be called "Operation Avalanche."

General Giuseppe Castellano negotiated the terms of the Italian surrender.

Germany reacted with "Operation Axis" the same day, when German troops entered Rome, forcing General Badoglio and the royal family to flee the city. Italian troops surrendered to their former allies or were shot if they showed any sign of resistance. The German navy also sunk the Italian battleship *Roma*, which was headed for an Allied-controlled port in North Africa. With it, more than 1,500 crewmen drowned. US President Franklin D. Roosevelt saw the surrender of Italy as a huge step towards victory, still knowing that the war was far from over. In a broadcast from Washington, he famously said, "The great news you have heard from General Eisenhower does not give you license to settle back in your rocking chair and say 'Well, that does it. We've got 'em on the run. Now we start celebrating.' The time has not yet come for celebration."

The Beginning of the End: From the Invasion of Salerno to the Battle of the Bulge

35) September 9, 1943 - Invasion of Salerno

One day after the Italian surrender, "Operation Avalanche" was launched. It marked the main invasion at Salerno. In order to surprise the Germans, army generals decided to attack without naval or aerial bombardment. The tactical move did not produce its intended effect, as the Wehrmacht already expected Allied troops in the region and stood prepared. Once the first wave of the US 36th Infantry Division approached the shore, an English voice could be heard saying: "Come on in and give up. We have you covered."

Landing of an Army Jeep at Salerno

Nevertheless, most Allied divisions accomplished their mission to secure their assigned sector.

Only two British infantry divisions met harsh resistance and had to fight their way ashore, supported by the help of naval bombs. Because of the intense German resistance, British commanders had to concentrate their forces and could not drive south as planned to join with the Americans. By the end of the first day, the Allied forces had advanced about five to seven miles (11.5 km) inland.

36) November 6, 1943 - Kiev Is Liberated By Soviet Troops

In November 1943, the Soviet troops further pushed back the Germans and liberated Kiev, the Ukrainian capital, from occupation. The offensive on the city started in October, with the main strike coming from the south. Unfortunately, all early attempts to break through to the city proved unsuccessful. Soviet generals then ordered to launch an offensive from different points, while keeping some formations south. They hoped to lead the Germans into thinking all of their troops were still there.

The trick worked, as on November 5, they were able to break into the city using the highway Brest-Litovsk. Thousands of foot soldiers and hundreds of tanks were soon ordered to take the same route and seize the rest of the city. By dawn the next day, enemy resistance was broken and during the next hours, Stalin received a message saying that Kiev was freed from the Nazis.

37) December 1, 1943 - Cairo Declaration

The Cairo Conference and the subsequent Cairo Declaration was an official announcement on behalf of the Allied powers of their intention to establish an international organization to maintain the peace and security in the world. President Franklin Roosevelt of the United States, Prime Minister Winston Churchill of the United Kingdom, and Generalissimo Chiang Kai-shek of the Republic of China met in November 1942 to discuss post-war order and goals.

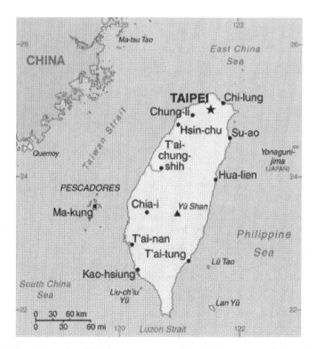

The island of Taiwan, near the Chinese mainland

The Cairo Declaration was no law itself, but a statement of intention. However, it did greatly affect the transfer of sovereignty of Taiwan to China after the war. When Japan surrendered on September 2, 1945, it specifically accepted the terms of the Potsdam Declaration, which referred to the terms of the Cairo Declaration. In it, the Japanese sovereignty after the war was to be limited to the islands of Honshu, Hokkaido, Kyushu, and Shikoku. This left out Taiwan, which China saw as legal evidence to incorporate the island under its government. Unclear lawmaking later led to various legal conflicts. In 1949, a CIA report claimed that Taiwan was not part of the Republic of China, stating, "Pending a Japanese peace treaty, the island remains occupied territory in which the US has proprietary interests."

38) June 6, 1944 - D-Day

On June 6, 1944, the Allied powers crossed the English Channel and landed on the beaches of Normandy, France. This event marked the beginning of the liberation of Western Europe from Nazi control. The plan was to further advance towards Germany, where British and American troops would meet up with Soviet forces moving in from the east. A successful invasion of the continent was central to winning the war, and both sides prepared for what was coming next. Hitler, long expecting an invasion in northwestern Europe, built up his troops in the region and hoped to repel any attacks and delay future invasion attempts.

Soldiers landing on Omaha Beach, the most deadly beach during D-Day

On the night of June 5, 18,000 parachutists headed for their drop zones in France. An additional 13,000 aircraft were mobilized to provide air cover and support for the invasion. The next morning, the land invasions began at 6:30 AM. Several beaches were split up between American, British, and Canadian forces. Opposition was light at Gold, Juno, and Sword beaches, and mediocre at Utah beach. Heavy resistance was encountered at Omaha Beach, where more than 2,000 troops were lost. Many soldiers later described the scenario as one of the biggest bloodbaths they had ever seen. Eventually, the beach was taken, enabling more troops and tanks to land. By the end of the day, 155,000 Allied troops had successfully stormed Normandy's beaches, while the German military suffered from confusion in its ranks. Hitler believed that the invasion was a feint to distract them from a coming attack north of the Seine River and ordered not to release nearby divisions to defend the beach. In addition, the Allies had destroyed many key bridges and forced the

Germans to take long detours. Towards the end of June, the Allies had almost a million soldiers and 150,000 vehicles in France, and were poised to continue their march across Europe.

39) August 25, 1944 - Liberation of Paris

Paris was liberated in August 1944 after more than four years of Nazi occupation. Before Allied troops reached the city, German General Dietrich von Choltitz received an order by Hitler to blow up Paris' landmarks and burn the city to the ground. He defied the order and signed a formal surrender. One day later, on August 26, Free French General Charles de Gaulle led a joyous liberation march down the Champs Élysées.

General de Gaulle and his entourage proudly stroll down the Champs Élysées.

At first, Allied generals decided to delay the liberation of the city in order not to divert valuable resources away from important operations elsewhere. Paris was to be encircled and then liberated at a later date. De Gaulle urged Eisenhower to reconsider, assuring him that Paris could be reclaimed without difficulty. He told his counterpart that if a liberation of Paris was not ordered, he would send his own troops into the city himself. Eisenhower then agreed to a conjunct attack on the city and deployed American forces the next day. Fights lasted only a couple days, and once the Germans were defeated, the Allied soldiers were greeted by enthusiastic civilians. De Gaulle later served from 1958 to 1969 as French president under the Fifth Republic.

40) October 20, 1944 - US Troops Land in the Philippines

In 1942, after the Japanese had taken the Philippines, United States General Douglas MacArthur promised to return and liberate the country. Two years later, he kept his promise and planned a land and sea operation to defeat the Japanese. More than a hundred thousand soldiers from US Sixth Army landed at Leyte, an island in the center of the Philippines, during the first wave on October 20. The battle at sea that began three days later would become the largest in history. 200,000 men and close to 300 ships would fight over a great part of the ocean.

US armored car during the attack

By the time the famous sea battle of Leyte Gulf was over, more than 30 ships and 10,000 men of the Japanese navy were destroyed and killed. American losses accounted for only six ships and 2,800 men. On land, resistance to the newly arrived American ground troops was significant. More than ten thousand Japanese troops already deployed were quickly reinforced by another 45,000. Bad terrain and rough weather also complicated American operations. It would take until the end of 1944 for the island to be entirely taken by US troops.

41) December 16, 1944 - Battle of the Bulge

The last German offensive to recapture the important harbor of Antwerp and big parts of Western Europe was the so-called Battle of the Bulge. Attacking in the Ardennes Forest in eastern Belgium on December 16, many hundreds of German tanks and more than a hundred thousand German troops were able to break through the thinly held American lines. Even though the Germans advanced as much as fifty miles in some areas, the Ardennes offensive was unsuccessful. US forces managed to hold back their enemy long enough to permit reinforcements to be moved into position and fight off the German drive. Only a few days later on December 26, it became clear that the German advance had been halted short of its objective.

German troops running past abandoned American equipment

In the face of increasing Allied pressure, German soldiers began to retreat from the Bulge in January the following year. As US Army Divisions met, their advance continued, taking back all German gains by the end of the month. Without stopping, US forces attacked the German positions along the Siegfried Line, which showed little defense after the heavy German losses during the Ardennes offensive. Towards the end of the Battle of the Bulge, German casualties amounted to more than 100,000, with American casualties at approximately 81,000.

The Defeat of the Axis: From the Invasion of Germany to the Atom Bomb

42) March 7, 1945 - US Troops Cross the Rhine River at Remagen

After the Allies had regained all the ground lost during the Battle of the Bulge, they resumed their advance into the Rhineland toward the Rhine River. It was the last natural barrier to Germany's heartland, and they planned to launch assaults across the Rhine at several locations during March. Wesel, a town north of the Ruhr, was chosen as the optimal location for crossing the river. However, before the infantry could attack, another division managed to capture a bridge further south. During the time of its capture, the Ludendorff Railroad Bridge at Remagen was one of the few bridges across the Rhine still standing. Armored infantry fought their way across under intense enemy fire as the Germans attempted to destroy it with demolition charges. A series of explosions damaged part of the bridge, though the main charges failed to go off and the iron framework remained intact.

The bridge in 1945 before its collapse

The rough terrain on the eastern bank of the Rhine at Remagen made the region a less than ideal avenue for the invasion of Germany.

Nevertheless, plans were quickly adjusted to take advantage of this coup. The Allies seized the opportunity to transport troops, tanks, and vehicles across the bridge, rather than over the river by boats. Many thousand men and vehicles crossed the bridge during the next days. On March 17, 1945, the Ludendorff bridge, severely damaged in the fighting ten days earlier and weakened further from the strain of heavy traffic, collapsed into the Rhine. As most of the Allied armies had crossed the Rhine already, they now prepared to drive into the interior of Germany.

43) April 16, 1945 - Soviets Encircle Berlin

The Battle for Berlin marked the end of World War II in Europe. Joseph Stalin had ordered his two most potent generals – Zhukov and Konev – to race to the city. Equipped with such an immense advantage in men, reaching the capital was comparatively easy, since the Wehrmacht was constantly retreating and the Red Army could use its forward momentum. Nonetheless, both generals knew that the battle for the actual city would be a very difficult one.

Soviet rocket launchers fire in Berlin

Despite the hopelessness of the situation, some German generals still showed faith for their 12th Army, which withdrew from the western front in order to help fight the Soviets. They knew that the amount of Russian tanks the Red Army sent meant little in the destroyed streets of Berlin. German soldiers who defended the city were given portable anti-tank explosives and used guerrilla tactics against their enemies. Land had to be taken street by street as the Germans held on to every inch. Death rates on both sides were enormous. Sometimes, the Russians would simply destroy an entire building if capturing it seemed too difficult or shots had been fired from within. The city of Berlin surrendered to the Russians on May 2, 1945. The Red Army had lost 80,000 men in the battle, almost 300,000 were wounded, and more than a thousand Russian tanks were destroyed. On the German side, things did not look much better. 150,000 Wehrmacht soldiers had lost their lives. After the fight, a photo of an infantry soldier raising the Red Flag on the top of the Reichstag, signaling the end of the war, gained worldwide fame.

44) April 30, 1945 - Suicide of Hitler

On April 30, 1945, one week before Germany would surrender to the Allied forces, Adolf Hitler committed suicide by shooting himself in the head. That afternoon, as noted in Hitler's last will, his remains were brought up the stairs through the bunker's exit and burnt in the Reich Chancellery garden outside. Russian archives show that his body was later recovered and interred in successive locations until 1970, when it was once again dug up, burnt, and the ashes scattered.

Front page of the US Armed Forces newspaper

In the beginning of 1945, with the Soviets closing in on Berlin, Hitler sought shelter in his bunker. Built just under the chancellery, it contained several rooms with self-sufficient electrical and water supply. Although many of his generals believed he had become mad, he continued in his position and gave orders. Meetings were held on a daily basis with German officials and war generals. Just two days before his suicide, he married Eva Braun, his longtime friend and mistress. In his testament, Hitler made Admiral Karl Donitz head of state. He then went to his private room, where Braun poisoned herself and their dogs and Hitler shot himself.

45) May 7, 1945 - Germany Surrenders to the Western Allies

On May 7, 1945, German General Alfred Jodl signed an unconditional surrender to the Allied forces at their headquarters in Reims, France. The surrender was to take effect the following day, ending the European conflict of World War II. The Germans had hoped to limit the conditions of surrender to just the Wehrmacht, which was fighting in the west, but due to the imminent failure of Nazi troops, they lost any leverage in asking for certain conditions. General Dwight Eisenhower declared that he expected the complete surrender of all Axis forces, and if this demand should not be met, the Allies were prepared to block their western front, which would leave German troops in the hands of the enclosing Soviet forces.

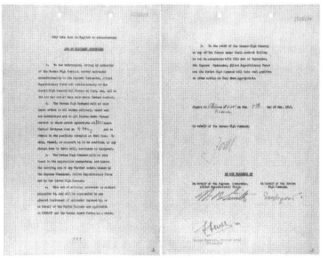

The German Instrument of Surrender

During the time of the signing, Jodl was not the highest official in the German Reich and therefore sent Admiral Karl Dönitz, Hitler's successor, the necessary information. Dönitz subsequently ordered him to sign. Both Jodl and Dönitz were convicted at the Nuremberg trials a year later. Jodl received the death sentence and Dönitz was convicted to ten years in military prison. May 8, the day after the signing, was declared Victory-in-Europe (V-E) Day, and is still celebrated as a public holiday in some European countries.

46) May 1945 - Demobilization of American Army Begins

The demobilization of the United States armed forces after the Second World War began with the defeat of Germany in May 1945 and continued until years later. During the war, the United States deployed more than 12 million men and women overseas. When Germany surrendered, still more than seven million troops were stationed abroad, three million of them in Europe. Soon, the public demanded a fast demobilization to bring the soldiers back home. Committees were established to solve this logistical problem, and official organization was given to the War Shipping Administration. Soldiers were then grouped into three categories: occupation, redeployment, or demobilization.

Rehabilitation Center for returned soldiers

All soldiers of the category "occupation" were to remain in Europe, in total more than 300,000 men. "Redeployment" units would be re-deployed to the Pacific to fight Japan.

Only "demobilization" units could return to the US and discharge. Even though this system worked well, some soldiers would have to wait months for transport. The military made it clear that the war in the Pacific had first priority.

47) July 16, 1945 - Atom Bomb Tested in New Mexico

The first ever detonation of a nuclear weapon was code-named Trinity. As part of the Manhattan Project, the US Army wanted to fire off a nuclear device with a similar design to the Fat Man bomb, which was later dropped over Nagasaki. The New Mexico desert was chosen as the ideal site for the test, and a base camp was built.

The mushroom cloud forming after the explosion

Leading up this event, more than a hundred of the top scientists in the US had worked five years to build a bomb based on a nuclear chain reaction. The initial budget in 1940 was just over $6,000, though this limit was removed once the US entered the war. On the morning of July 16, 120 miles south of Santa Fe, preparations were made to set off this giant bomb. In order to observe the explosion, scientists removed themselves 10,000 yards from the detonation point. As the bomb exploded, a mushroom cloud formed and the pillar on which the bomb was deposited was completely destroyed. Once reports of a successful detonation reached Washington D.C., the question remained as to if and where the bomb should be dropped. Germany was eliminated as the initial target, leaving only Japan.

48) August 6, 1945 - US Drops Atomic Bomb on Hiroshima

In 1940, the United States had been warned by Albert Einstein that Nazi Germany was conducting research into nuclear weapons. In order to avoid a defeat through this powerful weapon, the US started its own atomic weapon program. After five years, and by the time the first successful tests were conducted in 1945, the Germans had already surrendered. However, the war in the Pacific showed no end in sight. President Truman was told that any attempt to invade mainland Japan would result in tens of thousands of American casualties. It was then suggested that the new weapon could be used to end the war and spare American lives.

An Atomic cloud over Nagasaki

The American bomber Enola Gay headed for Hiroshima on August 6, 1945, where it dropped a five-ton bomb. The blast immediately killed 80,000 people, with tens of thousands dying in the following weeks from the radiation. On August 9, another bomb was dropped on the city of Nagasaki, killing almost 40,000 more people. President Truman then declared that if the Japanese did not accept US terms, they should "expect a rain of ruin from the air the like of which has never been seen on Earth." Historians now interpret this act as a demonstration of power not only to the Japanese, but also to the Soviets, as relations between them and the United States deteriorated badly towards the end of the war.

49) August 8, 1945 - Soviets Declare War on Japan

Between the first and the second atomic bomb, the Soviet Union officially declared war on Japan on August 8, 1945. Following the declaration of war, more than one million Soviet soldiers moved into Japanese-occupied Manchuria to face approximately 700,000

Japanese soldiers. Although the bombs destroyed Hiroshima and Nagasaki almost entirely, they did not have the desired effect. More than half of the Japanese Cabinet did not want to surrender unconditionally. This especially regarded the position of Hirohito the Japanese emperor. Public outcry was also less than expected, as news spread slowly and only a few Japanese civilians even knew of the bombs. Most of the inhabitants of Hiroshima and Nagasaki were either dead or suffering terribly.

Soviet Sailor hoisting the Soviet naval ensign

The Soviet Manchuria offensive stood in contrast to the American campaigns in the Pacific. Soviet generals launched a massive invasion right after declaring war, and the Red Army rapidly took over the region. The overwhelming success of the invasion was partly due to the fact that the Japanese did not expect to face the Soviets until 1946. They left many strategic points unprotected, making them easy to capture. After the devastating invasion, Japanese Emperor Hirohito pled with his War Council to reconsider surrender to spare his people.

50) September 2, 1945 - Japan Surrenders

By the summer of 1945, the defeat of Japan was only a matter of time. Both their navy and air force were unable to keep fighting, and the atomic bombs had destroyed two major cities. In the Potsdam Declaration, the Allies demanded the unconditional surrender of all Japanese armed forces and stated that if the country failed to comply, "complete destruction of the Japanese homeland" would be the consequence." Even though the Japanese government paid no attention to the Potsdam Declaration at first, this changed once the Soviet Union invaded Manchuria.

Mamoru Shigemitsu signing the Japanese Instrument of Surrender

Shortly after the attack, Japanese Emperor Hirohito spoke to the Supreme War Council. The Emperor suggested that it would be best to accept the Potsdam Declaration under the condition to keep his prerogatives as the sovereign Emperor. His suggestion was accepted by the council, and one day later, a message was sent to the United States. The American response was vague about the Japanese demands, a fact that Emperor Hirohito brushed aside, as he stated that he preferred peace to destruction. The USS *Missouri* was chosen as the site of Japan's formal surrender, and on Sunday, September 2, more than two hundred fifty Allied warships laid anchor in Tokyo. In the morning hours, Japanese Foreign Minister Mamoru Shigemitsu signed the Instrument of Surrender. Commander MacArthur signed on behalf of the United Nations with representatives from China, the USSR, Britain, and other Allied countries following him.

Other Books in the *History in 50 Events* Series

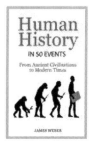

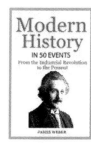

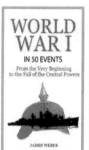

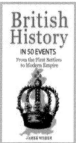

Made in the USA
Lexington, KY
21 September 2016